COUNTING BY

ONES

Kay Robertson

Rourke
Educational Media

rourkeeducationalmedia.com

Scan for Related Titles
and Teacher Resources

Teaching Focus:

Ending Punctuation - Have students locate the ending punctuation for sentences in the book. Count how many times a period, question mark, or exclamation point is used. Which one is used the most? What is the purpose for each ending punctuation mark? Practice reading these sentences with appropriate expression.

Before Reading:

Building Academic Vocabulary and Background Knowledge

Before reading a book, it is important to set the stage for your child or student by using pre-reading strategies. This will help them develop their vocabulary, increase their reading comprehension, and make connections across the curriculum.

1. Read the title and look at the cover. *Let's make predictions about what this book will be about.*
2. Take a picture walk by talking about the pictures/photographs in the book. Implant the vocabulary as you take the picture walk. Be sure to talk about the text features such as headings, Table of Contents, glossary, bolded words, captions, charts/diagrams, or Index.
3. Have students read the first page of text with you then have students read the remaining text.
4. Strategy Talk – use to assist students while reading.
   - Get your mouth ready
   - Look at the picture
   - Think…does it make sense
   - Think…does it look right
   - Think…does it sound right
   - Chunk it – by looking for a part you know
5. Read it again.
6. After reading the book complete the activities below.

High Frequency Words

Flip through the book and locate how many times the high frequency words were used.

count
have
my
on
ones
the
you
your

After Reading:

Comprehension and Extension Activity

After reading the book, work on the following questions with your child or students in order to check their level of reading comprehension and content mastery.

1. *Why is counting important?* (Asking questions)
2. *How many people are in the book?* (Summarize)
3. *How many animals are in the book?* (Summarize)
4. *How many shoes are in your home or classroom?* (Text to self connection)

Extension Activity

Now it's your turn to do some counting. Look around your home or classroom. With an adult, make a list of different objects you see such as coats, markers, backpacks, shoes, toy cars, or lights. Now go around the classroom and count! Write the number next to the item. How many coats do you see? How many markers did you find?

One, two
Let's count shoes!

Three, four
Shoes on the floor.

3

4

Five, six
Shoes on chicks.

Seven, eight
Find your shoe or we'll
be late.

Nine, ten
Where have these shoes been?

5 6 7 8 9 10

11

Eleven, twelve
Shoes sit neatly
on the shelves.

Thirteen, fourteen

Shoes are off for trampoline jumping.

Fifteen, sixteen

Are your shoes green?

Seventeen, eighteen

Everyone loves their shoes and jeans.

11 12 13 14 15 16 17 18

Nineteen, twenty

Now we have plenty.

Twenty-one, twenty-two

Can you help me find my shoes?

Index

Websites

http://pbskids.org/games/123/

http://www.primarygames.com/math/ fishycount/

http://www.ixl.com/math/kindergarten/ represent-numbers-up-to-20

Meet The Author!
www.meetREMauthors.com

About the Author

Kay Robertson loves all kinds of shoes. In fact, she has shoe Christmas tree ornaments and a whole book of shoe pictures. When she was young, she loved to wear her red boots that matched her super cool red bicycle.

www.rourkeeducationalmedia.com

PHOTO CREDITS: cover: chicks photo © stockphoto mania, cover shoes © d13, Svetislav1944;
colored numbers throughout © USBFCO; page 3 © Olha Ukhal; page 4, 5 © Karkas; page 6-7 © stockphoto mania, shoes © d13, Svetislav1944; page 8-9 © 2xSamara.com and Flashon Studio; shoe © Texturis; page 10-11 © forest badger, nonstick, Andrew Burgess, Jon Le-Bon, Olga Sapegina; page 13 © Africa Studio; page 14-15 © Ilike, Rawpixel, Ewa Studio; page 16-17 © Rawpixel, green tennis shoes © Jeka; page 18-19 © Andrea Slatter, michaeljung, Paul Matthew Photography, Hans Kim, Catalin Petole; page 20-21 © Kekyalyaynen, SchubPhoto, Ivonne Wierink, BNMK0819, Supertrooper, 3445128471, Patrick Foto; page 22-23 © In Green, Sergey Sukhorukov, Samuel Borges Photography; Kim Ruoff, Monkey Business Images, glenda, Paul Hakimata Photography, psnoonan, Flashon Studio, Gajus, Le Do

Edited by: Luana Mitten

Cover design and Interior design: by Nicola Stratford www.nicolastratford.com

Library of Congress PCN Data

Counting by Ones/ Kay Robertson
(Concepts)
ISBN 978-1-63430-055-1 (hard cover)
ISBN 978-1-63430-085-8 (soft cover)
ISBN 978-1-63430-113-8 (e-Book)
Library of Congress Control Numbe: 2014953333

Rourke Educational Media
Printed in the United States of America, North Mankato, Minnesota

Also Available as: